T0193286

LOGOTHERAPY FOR TEENS
WITH
EXPRESSIVE ARTS TECHNIQUES

GROUP THERAPY BOOK

JULIE L. QUIGLEY, PH.D., NCC, LMHC, SCHOOL COUNSELOR
COUNSELOR EDUCATOR | PRIVATE PRACTICE THERAPIST

WELCOME!

I have worked with adolescents who struggle with depression and self-identity for many years. Some of their identity struggles have been associated with their feelings of not having a purpose on earth. I decided to write this group counseling workbook to inspire other counselors to recognize the importance of acceptance and awareness of contributing to society. I incorporated expressive arts because this type of counseling aligns with Logotherapy and provides a space to express themselves through a different communication channel. This type of expression provides a safe and non-threatening way to explore their feelings and identity.

I want to think my daughters, Grace, Lillian, and Abigail, for being amazing and supporting me through this project, and let me know when I am just "off base."

Julie L. Quigley, Ph.D., NCC, LMHC, School Counselor
Counselor Educator | Private Practice Therapist

Copyright 2022
All Rights Reserved

To order additional copies of this book, contact:
Xlibris
844-714-8691
www.Xlibris.com
Orders@Xlibris.com

ISBN: Softcover   978-1-6698-2707-8
          EBook   978-1-6698-2706-1

Print information available on the last page

Rev. date: 05/23/2022

CONTENTS

LOGOTHERAPY & EXPRESSIVE ARTS

- Explain the theoretical backgrounds used to create the group counseling curriculum.
- Explain how to apply logotherapy with expressive arts group counseling in clinical settings.
- Describe the 8 session group counseling format.

FOUNDATIONAL RESEARCH

Research	Theorist	Primary Tenets	Technique	Outcomes of therapy
Identity development	D. J. Hacker	**4 Key conflicts** that Challenge Identity in Early Adolescence: Isolation, Death, Choice, Meaning	Existential processing questions that address identity development	Social connectedness, sense of purpose, and emotion regulation
Logotherapy	Viktor Frankl	**3 Natures of the human mind:** Freedom of Will, Will to Meaning, Meaning of Life **Existential vacuum** can develop when adolescents do not see meaning in their life.	Existential analysis, Socratic dialogue, Creativity, Discovering Meaning, Logoanchor	Discovering identity, autonomy, self-awareness, connectedness to the world, purpose on earth
Expressive Arts	Natalie Rogers	**The Creative Connection** Express inner feelings by creating outer forms	Safe environment, holistic, humanistic approach in the group counseling session	Explore existential themes in a non-prescribed manner, discover a sense of meaning in life, and develop inner strength to face the future

FOUNDATIONAL RESEARCH CONTINUED

Research	Theorist	Primary Tenets	Technique	Outcomes of therapy
3H model: Head Heart, & Hands	Warren, Lerner, Phelps, Spiewak, & Sherrod, 2011	3H model hypothesizes three centric domains of functioning common to positive youth development and religion/spirituality: **Head**- Cognitive **Heart**- Affective **Hands**- Psychomotor	Incorporate **Cognitive** (head), **Affective** (heart), and **Psychomotor** (engagement) techniques to development and promote internal and external assets.	Emotional satisfaction and personal effectiveness by projecting a sense of one's "true self "; self-reflection, self-concept, and being active in a meaningful manner
Religious conversion and Adolescent development	Spilka, Hood, Hunsberger, & Gorsuch, 2003 Clintton and Hawkins, 2011	Adolescence by virtue of its special qualities is considered a likely period for conversion. The place of doubt in religious identity may provide a meaningful experience in identify formation.	**Socratic questions** and recognizing protective religious resources within the identity formation activities	Provides a moral meaning system and community connectedness and identity to channel positive youth development. The questions and issues raised by existentialism align with the Bible.

GROUP DESIGN

Session Norms

Ultimate Coping Playlist
Each session the group will share a song from the playlist worksheet. The facilitator will collect all the songs from each session and create a group master playlist and play and share with each member of the counseling group on the last group session. This provides group cohesiveness and is a modified LogoAnchor technique

Logo Journey Journal
Participants will keep a journal of their logotherapy experience and answer the questions provided. This deepens the participants, self-discovery and tracks what they have learned, observed, and overcome that particular week.

Socratic Dialogue
Socratic dialogue processing questions are listed for each session. This is logotherapy's main tool to spark dialogue in order to find meaning through self-introspection, self-discovery, choice, uniqueness, responsibility, accountability, and self-transcendence.

Session Snapshot

Session Timeframe
Each session is set up to run for 90 minutes.

Scrapbook
Each session will have an activity that can be added to the participants' scrapbooks. Thrdr scrapbookd will be shared and reflected upon in the last group session.

Session 1
Introduction
Name Art
Socratic Dialogue

Session 2
Explore Identity
My Social Footprint
Socratic Dialogue

Session 3
Explore Identity Continued
Visual Arts/Phototherapy
Dereflection
Socratic Dialogue

Session 4
Life and Meaning
Dereflection &
LogoAncher
Recycle Your Heart
Socratic Dialogue

Session 5
Pursue Meaning
Tattoo
Self-Transcendence
Socratic Dialogue

Session 6
Values
Values Compass
Values Collage
Socratic Dialogue

Session 7
Authentic Goals
SMART Goals
Self-Transcendence
Socratic Dialogue

Session 8
Process the Journey
Logo Journey Journal
Master Copying
Playlist
Socratic Dialogue

INTRODUCTION TO GROUP

OBJECTIVES

- Enable group members to meet, learn about the group process, and expressive arts modalities.
- Build rapport with the group members and leader.
- Create group rules and create a safe space.
- Introduction to logotherapy and expressive arts.

NAME ART

Purpose and Goals

The goal of the first group session is for the leader to discuss the group norms, explain the group process, introduce logotherapy and expressive arts modalities, and build a safe and creative environment so members feel comfortable being themselves and learn, about one another.

Getting Acquainted Activity

Group leaders can begin the session by introducing themselves, saying why they enjoy using expressive arts and logotherapy, and asking participants if they have questions or reservations at the moment. Then, using a large poster board and markers, the group leaders ask the members to list guidelines or expectations they have to make the group sessions a safe space. The leaders write the comments and create a consensus for the group norms. Make sure to address confidentiality, respecting one another, no-judgment zone, and being on time. Revisit the rules at any time throughout the group process.

- Have group members create their names on a piece of paper using the art materials in a way that is meaningful to them.
- Next, have them add pictures, words, phrases, etc. on how their name was given to them.

Processing and Wrapping it Up

Have each member share their name art in the group. Then, ask the processing questions. Take time to review the group norms and introduce that each week you will start the session with a favorite song. In Session 2 each group member will share a **favorite song** and explain why it's their favorite. Assign a journal entry to their **Logo Journey Journal.**

MATERIALS

- Group rules template
- My Ultimate Coping Playlist
- Large poster board
- Markers
- Basic art supplies
- Blank white paper
- Colored construction paper
- Crayons
- Pencils

PROCESSING QUESTIONS

- What was it like to create your name art?
- Does your name have a special meaning in your religion?
- Do you think your name fits your personality?
- What part of your name or how you got your name makes you proud?
- What commonalities and differences did you notice while the members were sharing?
- What was it like to see other group members, name art?

SESSION 2

EXPLORE IDENTITY

OBJECTIVES

- Understand the concept of identity.
- Gain awareness of how religious or spiritual formation informs their identity.
- Gain awareness of their social media identity and compare it to their desired identity.

MY SOCIAL MEDIA FOOTPRINT

Purpose and Goals
The goal of this activityis to help the clients understand the concept of identity and evaluate if their social media identity is the same as their desired identity. Who does the world think they are? Whom do they want to be?

Social Media Activity
Group leaders will begin the session by greeting all group members and having each member share their **favorite song** and why it's a favorite.

- Explain the concept of identity and why this is an integral part of our existence as human beings.
- Have group members write down all the social media accounts they have.
- Next, have them review their accounts and complete the **My Social Footprint Worksheet**.
- Group members can share their identities on social media.

Processing and Wrapping it Up
Have members share what their social footprint says about them. Then, discuss the processing questions.

- Add the worksheet to their group scrapbook.
- Prep the group for the Star News! Phototherapy assignment by giving each member a disposable camera.
- They are like paparazzi stalking themselves and taking pictures of meaningful people and places to capture all elements of their lives.
- Tell the clients to develop the film before the next session. The therapist should tell the parents to help with this as well.
- Ask the group to share a **song** they associate with **freedom** in the next session.
- Assign a journal entry to their **Logo Journey Journal**.

MATERIALS

- Client's phone
- Social media handles
- Writing utensil
- Disposable camera for each member of the group.

PROCESSING QUESTIONS

- Who does the world think you are?
- What evidence on your social media accounts shows this identity?
- Why should you care what your social media accounts say about you?
- Does your social footprint match the person you want to be?
- Do you have different identities on different social media accounts? Why?

My Social Footprint

Who does your social footprint say you are?

Name _____ My Social Media Accounts

Events My Social Media Accounts Show in My Life

Date	Event
_____	_____
_____	_____
_____	_____
_____	_____
_____	_____
_____	_____
_____	_____
_____	_____
_____	_____
_____	_____

My Social Media Personality/Characteristics

_____	_____
_____	_____
_____	_____
_____	_____
_____	_____
_____	_____
_____	_____
_____	_____

SESSION 3

EXPLORE IDENTITY
CONTINUED

OBJECTIVES

- Continue the journey of self-discovery.
- An exercise to reflect on their life circumstances and experiences to help them put things in perspective.
- Identify personal values and significant objects and people in their life.
- Process how their religious life impacts their identity.

STAR NEWS!

Purpose and Goals

The goal of this activity is for the group members to identify their strengths, challenges, and personal values to create their personal story through phototherapy. The group members will explore significant places, people, and things that contribute to their identity. Also, this session helps the members gain awareness of how life experiences shape how they view the world.

Star News Activity

Group leaders will begin the session by greeting all group members and having each member share a **song** they associate with **freedom**.

- Review phototherapy and how it can be used to create their personal story. Have each member choose two scrapbook pages. I like to have many different options for members.
- One page will be the cover sheet for their magazine of choice, and one will be the photo story sheet.
- Pass out the worksheet with the different themes for them to create captions for their pictures.
- Then, have the members paste the pictures and write the captions on scrapbook paper.
- Have members decorate with other art supplies if they desire.
- Encourage members to be creative with their pages and use them to create their personal stories however they like.
- Have members create a title and cover page for their scrapbook that encompasses their life.

Processing and Wrapping it Up

Discuss the processing questions and allow group members to share their story with the group, if they like. Assign the group for the next session to share a **song** that makes them **sad** and why. Assign a journal entry to their **Logo Journey Journal**.

MATERIALS

- Photos
- Scrapbook pages
- Pens
- Markers
- Stickers
- Magazines
- Basic art supplies

PROCESSING QUESTIONS

- Does your magazine story differ from your social media self?
- How are you portrayed in your photos?
- Who or what is the biggest influence in your life?
- What are your biggest accomplishments ?
- Who are the most valued people in your life?
- Did you have any religious influencers in your life?
- How does religion or spirituality inform your personal story, if at all?

STAR NEWS!

STAR: _____

Strengths

_____
_____
_____
_____
_____
_____
_____

_____
_____
_____
_____
_____
_____

▲ Support System

Hobbies

_____
_____
_____
_____
_____
_____

STAR NEWS!

STAR: _____

Home 🏠	
	▲ **Favorite Places** 📷
School 📓	

LIFE AND MEANING

OBJECTIVES

- Identify positive and negative characteristics and behaviors in self and others.
- Incorporate a **LogoAnchor** technique by using music and imagery to connect a rich experience as an anchor in a current situation.
- Recognize how their religious beliefs inform how they view reconciliation and forgiveness.
- Evaluate meaning and meaninglessness in life.

RECYCLE YOUR HEART

Purpose and Goals

The goal of this activity is to develop positive and negative characteristics and events that inform their identity, provide self-reflection, and gain an understanding of how their religious or spiritual beliefs inform their heart and life.

Recycle Your Heart Activity

Group leaders will begin the session with each group member stating their name again and sharing a **song** that makes them **sad** and why.

- Each member receives a piece of construction and cuts a large heart by folding the paper in half lengthwise and drawing one side of a heart, then cutting it out.
- Have them break their heart by drawing zigzag lines or sections of the heart with your non-dominant hand make as many breaks in your heart as they have experienced in their lifetime.
- Then, write down the name or symbols of these heartbreaks with the non-dominant hand. This will be tricky.
- Write down characteristics that they do not like about themselves in their broken heart. Encourage them to be creative.
- Next, have them color the broken heart with their non-dominant hand. Make it as ugly as possible.
- Ask the processing questions about making the broken heart.
- Collect the broken hearts and keep for the next counseling session.

MATERIALS

- Construction paper
- Scrapbook pages
- Crayons
- Glue
- Scissors
- Sharpies
- Colored pens
- Wrapping paper cut in small squares (30) of different colors.
- Basic are supplies

PROCESSING QUESTIONS

Broken Heart

- What was it like to use your non-dominant hand?
- What were you feeling when you listed your heartbreaks and made your heart ugly?
- Do you believe people can learn from their life experiences? Why?
- What is your religious or spiritual belief about people or negative events in life?

RECYCLE YOUR HEART, CONTINUED

- Have the clients collect their broken hearts from the last counseling session.
- **LogoAnchor Technique:** Now have the participants listen to calming music, close their eyes, feel what is tense in their body, and relax their muscles. Vision experiences, images, and events in their life that are happy and fill them with a sense of uniqueness.
- Then, have them write positive these things on a piece of tissue wrapping paper. This could be positive about themselves, life situations, friends, school, etc.
- Once each member has written several experiences, characteristics, etc., on their tissue wrapping paper, have them crumple each piece and glue it however they like to cover their broken heart.
- They should cover and decorate the heart with tissue paper however they like.
- Ask the processing questions regarding their recycled heart.

Processing and Wrapping it Up

Review how relaxation and LogoAnchor were employed with expressive arts to revive their meaningful experiences and positive view of themselves in the conscious mind. Assign a **song** that makes them feel **anxious** next session. Assign a journal entry to their Logo Journey Journal.

MATERIALS

- Construction paper
- Scrapbook pages
- Crayons
- Glue
- Scissors
- Sharpies
- Colored pens
- Tissue wrapping paper cut in small squares (30) of different colors.
- Basic art supplies

PROCESSING QUESTIONS

Recycled Heart

- Was it harder to list your positive characteristics? Why or why not?
- Which heart do you feel more comfortable in?
- Do your religious/spiritual beliefs (if any) say about a person's heart ? Can it change?
- Do you believe your life experiences shape who you are today?

SESSION 5

PURSUE MEANING

OBJECTIVES

- Discover and pursue the meaning of suffering or struggling through self-transcendence.
- Describe how this meaning relates to their spiritual beliefs.
- Gain awareness of the meaning of their suffering and how it is part of their identity.

"MAN IS NOT FREE FROM CONDITIONS, HE HAS THE ABILITY TO CHOOSE HIS ATTITUDE TOWARDS THESE CONDITIONS"
~FRANKL (1967, P. 19)

TATTOO

Purpose and Goals

The goal of this activity is for the members to gain the ability to transcend their situation to understand life's meaning and gain a sense of purpose in life, to understand how suffering provides meaning and is part of their identity.

Tatoo Activity

Group leaders begin the session by greeting all group members and having each member share a **song** that makes them feel **anxious** and why.

- Set the counseling session stage by telling them they are in a tattoo parlor choosing their tattoo with friends.
- Pass out the tracing paper to each member.
- Each member will use the tracing paper to draw a primary tattoo that symbolizes a struggle/suffering they have experienced in their life.
- Provide printed sheets from the internet, copies from a magazine or book with symbols, and provide their meaning of the symbol.
- Then, have them draw another tattoo on the same paper that symbolizes a meaning they gained from that struggle or suffering.

Processing and Wrapping It Up

Discuss the processing questions. Allow enough time to allow those in the group who would like to share their tattoos and their meaning. Assign a **song** to share next session that reminds them of a **good memory** and why. Also, have the members bring anything from home they would like to add to a collage for next session. Assign a journal entry to their **Logo Journey Journal**.

MATERIALS

- Tracing paper
- Printed symbols and meanings
- Scrapbook pages
- Pens
- Pencils
- Colored pencils
- Art supplies

PROCESSING QUESTIONS

- Why did you choose your primary tattoo?
- How did you feel while you were drawing your tattoo?
- How does your tattoo relate to your religious or spiritual beliefs?
- Do you want anyone to see your tattoo?

SESSION 6

VALUES

OBJECTIVES

- Self-assess their values in eight dimensions of their lives through questioning and evaluating.
- Discover how a person's values add meaning to life and purpose.
- Facilitate the process of self-reflection through expressive arts.

VALUES COLLAGE

Purpose and Goals

The goal of this activity is to determine values, increase the participants' insight into what they value, and gain an understanding of how they use their values and beliefs to make decisions. This technique is also used to reflect on personal values, and values of their family (introspection), and to increase cultural awareness.

Compass Activity

Group leaders begin the session by greeting all group members and having each member share a **song** that reminds them of a **good memory**.

- The group leader should pass out the scrapbook paper, art supplies, and magazines, and have the members get out anything they brought from home.
- Pass out the Values Compass worksheets.
- Have them take about 10-20 minutes to complete both sheets to discover their values.
- Have the participants create their Values Collage without limitations.

Dimension of Values Discussed:

- Family
- Romantic relationships
- Friends
- Hobbies
- School
- Spirituality
- Community
- Health

Processing and Wrapping It Up

Discuss the processing questions. Allow time for those group members who would like to share their values and beliefs with the group. Assign a **song** they like to **wake up to in the morning** to share for the next session. Assign a journal entry in their **Logo Journey Journal.**

MATERIALS

- Values Compass Worksheets
- Magazines
- Scrapbook paper
- Printed images
- Printed words
- Stickers
- Markers
- Glue

PROCESSING QUESTIONS

- Do yourvvalues come from a place of "should" or authenticity?
- Do you feel your upbringing impacts your chosen values?
- How does religion inform your values?
- Was it hard to find images and words to add?
- Do you bring your values into everyday decisions?
- Do you display these values as part of your branding/identity on social media or in person?
- Are you known for your values?

VALUES COMPASS

Values are things that are most important to you. They inform your decision-making consciously and unconsciously.

Write down the most important things to you in each category.

For example, if honesty is one of the most important things to you in a romantic relationship, write "honesty" in the romantic relationship category.

1 - FAMILY	5 - SCHOOL
2 - ROMANTIC RELATIONSHIPS	6 - SPIRITUALITY
3 - FRIENDS	7 - COMMUNITY
4 - HOBBIES	8 - HEALTH

VALUES COMPASS QUESTIONS

☐ **Family**
What is something that makes your family unique?

☐ **Romantic Relationships**
Describe your best relationship and what makes it so good.

☐ **Friends**
Describe one of your close friends. How would your close friends describe you?

☐ **Leisure**
If you had no responsibilities or commitments for one day, what would you do?

☐ **School**
Is school a priority? How do you feel about your current grades? Why?

☐ **Spirituality or Religion**
What is your religion? Whom do you believe made people and the Earth? How important is this to you on a scale of 1–10 (10 being most important)?

☐ **Community**
If you could send a message to your community, what would you say or do?

☐ **Health**
Do you exercise? How much? Do you try to eat healthily? How often?

NOTES

_____

_____

_____

_____

_____

_____

_____

_____

SESSION 7

GOALS

OBJECTIVES

- Discover how a person's values and experiences help create future goals.
- Determine authentic goals that are aligned with their values and provide meaning to their lives.
- Incorporate logotherapy's **self-transcendence** in creating personal goals.

GOALS

Purpose and Goals

The goal of this activity is to develop authentic goals by using personal beliefs and values to gain self-transcendence. Group members determine goals compatible with their values to create meaning in their life.

Goal Setting

Group leaders begin the session by greeting all group members and have them share a **song** that helps them **wake up in the morning** and why. Pass out the **Authentic Goals** worksheet and ask the participants to create **SMART** goals. Discuss how human beings have the freedom to make choices and respond to events.

Discuss **self-transcendence** as a shift in focus from the self to others, in values from extrinsic motivation, such as materialism, to intrinsic motivation (the activity itself is the reward). Self-transcendence can be an increase in one's moral campus (Wong, 2017). How does one increase a moral compass?

Have them review their scrapbook and each session's artwork to create goals aligned with their values. This can be a goal in any dimension of life and will be more authentic because it is from a meaning-oriented focus.

   S – **Specific**: What do I want to happen?
   M – **Measurable**: How will I know when I have achieved my goal?
   A – **Attainable**: Is the goal realistic and how will I accomplish it?
   R – **Realistic**: Why is my goal important to me?
   T – **Timely**: What is my timeframe for this goal?

Processing and Wrapping It Up

Discuss the processing questions. Allow time for thoses who would like to share their goals with the group. Assign the group a **song** that reminds them of **being loved**. Assign a journal entry to their **Logo Journey Journal.**

MATERIALS

- Authentic Goals Worksheet
- General art supplies
- Extra sheets of white paper.
- Scrapbook of all the activities completed in the group.

PROCESSING QUESTIONS

- Reflect on your goals and aspirations. Do they involve something or someone other than yourself?
- What does self-transcendence mean to you?
- How might you modify your goals to reach self-transcendence?
- What are a few changes you can make to your goals to expand your focus?
- Do you have religious or spiritual goals listed? Why or why not?

AUTHENTIC GOALS

Create vital goals and increase positive emotions. Review your values and create a goal that is aligned with your values. This can be a goal in any dimension of your life and will be more authentic because it is from a meaning-oriented focus.

SPECIFIC

What do I want to happen?

MEASUREABLE

How will I know when I have achieved my goal?

ATTAINABLE

Is the goal realistic and how will I accomplish it?

RELEVANT

Why is my goal important to me?

TIMELY

What is my timeframe for this goal?

SESSION 8

PROCESS THE JOURNEY

OBJECTIVES

- Process each member's identity journey through the Logotherapy Journey Journal discussions.
- Review how each member has grown in their Identity development.
- Gain awareness of how their religious or spiritual life informs their identity.
- Conclude and review the Ultimate Coping Playlist.

YOUR PERSONAL JOURNEY CONTINUES

Purpose and Goals

The goal of this last session is to process the journey of identity development and reflect upon the group counseling journey. This is a time when the group members discover how they portray themselves on social media, and whom they want to be moving forward.

Journey Continues Activity

Have each member of the group share a song that reminds them of being loved. Add the songs to the master playlist of the collected songs from the group's coping skills theme each week.

Ask the group to discuss their group journey by reviewing the **Logo Journey Journal and Scrapbook** and have participants share their most significant takeaway from the group.

Talk about how people's identity changes throughout their lifetime. The group members provide some relevant examples of how their identity has changed and why. Also, look for videos on the search for identity by famous people to whom your member population can relate; show the movie, and discuss parallels. Discuss whether they feel their identity aligns with how they see themselves in 5 years.

Processing and Wrapping It Up

Discuss the processing questions and encourage those who would like to share their thoughts about the group. The facilitator will share the master playlist of all the shared songs from the entire group and send it to all the group members.

MATERIALS

- Compiled individual scrapbook of group sessions
- Collected group playlist
- Logo Journey Journal

PROCESSING QUESTIONS

- What was your best part of the group?
- Did you find it easier to discuss and search your identity through expressive arts?
- What do you think the group can improve upon?
- What did you learn about yourself?
- Do you feel your identity has changed from the first session to now?
- Do you feel less anxious about who you are?
- Are you the person you want to be?
- How do you feel about the future?

REFERENCES

Baumel, W. T., & Constantino, J. N. (2020). Implementing logotherapy in slts second half-century: incorporating existential considerations into personalized treatment of adolescent depression. *Journal of the American Academy of Child & Adolescent Psychiatry,* 59(9), 1012-1015. https://doi.org/10.1016/j.jaac.2020.06.006

Blair, R. G. (2004). Helping older adolescents search for meaning in depression. Journal of Mental Health Counseling, 26(4), 333-347. https://doi.org/10.17744/mehc.26.4.w8u9h6uf5ybhapyl
Clinton, T., & Hawkins, R. (2011). T*he Popular Encyclopedia of Christian Counseling: An Indispensable Tool for Helping People with Their Problems.* Harvest House Publishers.

Dezelic, M. S., Ghanoum Psyd, G. (2015). *Meaning-Centered Therapy Manual: Logotherapy and Existential Analysis Brief Therapy Protocol for Group and Individual Sessions.* United States: Dezelic & Associates, Incorporated.

Dickson, C. (1975). Logotherapy as a pastoral tool. *Journal of Religion & Health,* 14(3), 207-213. https://doi.org/10.1007/BF01534049

Force, V. (2019). *Art therapy as a tool for enhancing adolescent Identity formation, self-knowing, and empowerment* (Publication No. 162) [Doctoral dissertation, Lesley University]. Digital Commons. https://digitalcommons.lesley.edu/expressive_theses/162

Frankl, Victor (1967). *Psychotherapy and Existentialism.* New York, NY: Washington Square Press.

Jahanpour, Z., Sareghin, S. A., Hosseini, F. S., & Tekiyee, A. (2014). The study of group logo-therapy effectiveness on self-esteem, happiness and social sufficiency in Tehranian girl teenagers. *Journal of Medical Sciences.* 7(3), 477-489.

Levine, E. G., Levine, S. K. (1998). *Foundations of expressive arts therapy: Theoretical and clinical perspectives.* United Kingdom: Jessica Kingsley Publishers.

Lindsey, L., Robertson, P., & Lindsey, B. (2018). Expressive arts and mindfulness: Aiding adolescents in understanding and managing their atress. *Journal of Creativity in Mental Health,* 13(3), 288-297. https://doi.org/10.1080/15401383.2018.1427167

Lowenstein, L. (Ed.). (2011). *Favorite therapeutic activities for children, adolescents, and families: Practitioners share their most effective interventions.* Champion Press.

Mannion, M. P. (2017). Existential Theory. In S. Degges-White & N. L. Davis (Eds.), *Integrating the expressive arts into counseling practice* (pp. 93-114). Springer Publishing Company. https://doi.org/10.1891/9780826177025.0006

Nelson, J. M., & McMillion, P. L. R. (2017). Neuroscientific Applications for Expressive Therapies. In S. Degges-White & N. L. Davis (Eds.), Integrating the expressive arts into counseling practice. Springer Publishing Company. https://doi.org/10.1891/9780826177025.0014

Price, E. W., & Swan, A. M. (2020). Connecting, coping, and creating: An expressive arts group for first year college students. *Journal of Creativity in Mental Health,* 15(3), 378-392. https://doi.org/10.1080/15401383.2019.1685924

Şanlı, E., & Ersanli, K. (2020). The effects of psycho-education program based on logotherapy for the development of a healthy sense of identity in emerging adulthoods. *Current Psychology.* https://doi.org/10.1007/s12144-020-01009-3

Warren, A.E.A., Lerner, R.M., Phelps, E., Spiewak, G.S. and Sherrod, L.R. (2011). The shared pathways of religious/spiritual engagement and positive youth development. *In Thriving and Spirituality Among Youth* (eds A.E.A. Warren, R.M. Lerner and E. Phelps). https://doi.org/10.1002/9781118092699.ch8

Wong, P. T. P. (2017b). Logotherapy. In A. Wenzel (Ed.), *The SAGE encyclopedia of abnormal and clinical psychology* (pp. 1984).

LOGO JOURNEY JOURNAL

L   **Learned About Myself**

_____

_____

_____

O   **Observed During Group**

_____

_____

_____

G   **Gained Insight About Myself or Others**

_____

_____

_____

O   **Overcame This Week**

_____

_____

_____

OTHER REFLECTIONS

_____

_____

_____

_____

_____

Group Rules

 Let's start the group by being on time, every time!

 What's said in the group, stays in the group.

 Respect others' opinions. No judgment.

 You can pass if you want to.

 Openness and honesty.

Recycle Your Heart

Pain is not wasted, it can be recycled.

"Face your life, its pain, its pleasure, leave no path untaken."
~ Neil Gaiman

MY ULTIMATE COPING PLAYLIST

We go through different positive and negative emotions every day. It is okay to have all those feelings, but we must also find ways to cope.

Fill the boxes with the titles of songs (and their artists) that you think fit the descriptions provided.

FOR FUN

---
a song that gets stuck in my head

---
a song I know all the words to

---
a song from my favorite movie or TV series

TO UPLIFT

---
a song I associate with freedom

---
a song that gives me energy

---
a song I'd like to wake me up

FOR FREEDOM

---
a song that makes me feel safe

---
a song that helps me think positively

---
a song that makes me feel independent

EMOTIONS I ENDURE

---
a song for when you get anxious worried

---
a song for when you get angry or annoyed

---
a song for when you feel lonely or afraid

POSITIVE EMOTIONS

---
a song that reminds you of a good memory

---
a song that makes you think of a loved one

---
a song to remind you that you are loved

Printed in the United States
by Baker & Taylor Publisher Services